TABLE OF

A NOTE FROM
THE AUTHOR

"The capacity to learn is a gift; the ability to learn is a skill; the willingness to learn is a choice." —Brian Herbert

Friends — I want to take a moment to say "Thank You" for joining me to learn about this incredible investment strategy. This book published in 2015 with no expectation that anyone other than friends and family would read it.

I've been overwhelmed by the positive reviews, comments, and emails from thousands of readers. I am humbled and honored to have helped so many others. I sincerely hope that you will be someone that is helped by something written in these pages.

Before we start, I want to make a few promises to you:

1. I promise to keep it simple. Investing theories can be complicated with lots of fancy-sounding words.

I'll try to avoid using investment jargon and explain investment concepts as simply as possible.

If you're already an advanced investor, you may be bored by some of the explanations. Please show me some grace here. I want this book to be accessible to everyone — regardless of previous investment knowledge or experience. Feel free to skip ahead if you're already well familiar with one of the topics.

2. I promise to be as brief as possible. I'll keep things short and sweet. I want you to quickly and easily get the information you want and move on with life. The average reader should be able to complete this entire book in just about the same time it takes you to mow your lawn.

With that in mind, please know that this is not a comprehensive book. This book is to introduce you to dividend growth investing as a strategy. It's not a Ph.D. dissertation on stock selection or financial statement analysis. If you're already well-versed in dividend growth investing — this book isn't for you. Please do not buy it. Or return it if you've already bought it.

If you're new to dividend growth investing, I think you'll find a lot of great information in these pages.

If I keep my end of the bargain, I'd like to ask a few things of you as the reader.

1. Have an open mind. Some of what I say in this book may completely contradict what you've previously learned about investing. That's OK. The strategy outlined in these pages turns some conventional investment wisdom on its head.

2. Don't over-complicate things. Wall Street and the financial services industry has a vested interest in making investing sound complicated. The dividend strategy is refreshingly simple. Don't dismiss it because it doesn't sound as fancy as other strategies you've read about. Dividend growth investing may be simple, but the long-term results are incredibly powerful.

3. Don't be shy! Few people make much money writing books. The biggest reward most authors get (me included) is hearing from you.

   At the end of this book, I'll provide my email address. If you enjoyed the book, let me know about it. If you wanted to read more about a particular topic, let me know about that also. If you hated the book, well, let me know what you didn't like about it.

Also, a few housekeeping items before we get going. You should know that I work for an investment firm that specializes in building dividend portfolios for clients.

Many of the principles in this book are consistent with the firm's investment strategy. However, this book is not affiliated with the firm that I work for in any way.

The information in this book should be considered education only. None of this material should be considered investment advice or a recommendation to buy any stock or asset. It's certainly not a substitute for consulting with a qualified financial professional.

Now that we've gotten those things out of the way, let's get started! I hope you enjoy the book and, most importantly, learn a thing or two that can help on your investment journey.

Blessings,

Nathan Winklepleck, CFA®

INTRODUCTION

"Investing should be more like watching paint dry or watching grass grow. If you want excitement. Take $800 and go to Las Vegas." –Paul Samuelson

This book will take you approximately 73 minutes to read from start to finish. I believe these could be the most valuable hour and 13 minutes of your life. Financially speaking, that is.

I want to introduce you to the most powerful investment strategy off all-time. No other investing approach combines consistent returns with below-average risk and simplicity. If you can find a strategy that does all of these things better, I would like to be the first one to know about it.

With this strategy, I believe you will be able to improve your future investment results by at least 1% per year. What would an additional 1% mean for you? If you invest $1,000 per month for the next 30 years, an extra 1% return is worth about $185,000. If you are starting with $500,000 today, an extra 1% would be worth $1 million in 30 years.

Since this book is only going to take you 73 minutes to read, you're currently on track to earn at least $2,534.35 per minute. So kick back, relax, and enjoy!

The Sad Reality for the Average Investor

From 1871 through 2016, the stock market produces a compounded return of 9.07% per year. That's enough to grow $1 into $319,492. No typos.

From 2009 to 2017, the US stock market — as measured by the S&P 500 Index — has increased in value by 260%. That's a 15.3% annualized return.

Most financial advisors will tell you they expect the same return to continue into the future. However, I wouldn't count on it. The combination of ultra-low interest rates, ultra-easy monetary policy, and low inflation have allowed stock prices to outpace underlying earnings and dividend growth for years.

In the future, returns are likely to be more muted. Far less than the 15% per year we've enjoyed since 2009. And probably worse than the market's long-term 9% return.

According to Vanguard, US stocks are likely to produce between 5% and 8% per year over the next decade. Bonds are likely to produce between 2% and 3.5%.

If you're following the classic "balanced" fund of 60% stocks and 40% bonds — your return will be between 3.8% and 6.2% per year. That's before fees. And — more importantly — before investor mistakes.

Fees

Let's talk fees for a minute. Most Americans invest in actively managed mutual funds. The average mutual fund charges 1.2% per year. That's not including any additional fees — including sales loads, 12b-1 fees, commissions, or other charges.

By the time you subtract management fees, the best case annual return for most investors is between 2.6% and 5% per year.

However, investment fees aren't the most important factor in your future returns. The biggest issue you will face as an investor? It's looking you in the mirror.

Behavioral Mistakes

Each year, research firm Dalbar releases a study of how actual investors are doing with managing their own portfolios. As of Dalbar's 2016 investment report, the average equity investor did worse than the S&P 500 by approximately 2.9% per year.

According to Dalbar, the biggest enemy to investor returns is not fees. Of the 2.9% underperformance, only 0.8% was directly attributable to management fees. A whopping 2.1% per year was because of their own mistakes.

"Investor behavior is not simply buying and selling at the wrong time, it is the psychological traps, triggers and misconceptions that cause investors to act irrationally. That irrationality leads to buying and selling at the wrong time, which leads to underperformance."—Dalbar's 2016 Quantitative Analysis of Investor Behavior.

If we assume the average investor repeats this performance in the future, we can subtract another 2.1% per year off of the 10-year return projections from Vanguard. That gets us to somewhere between 0.5% and 2.9% per year.

Inflation

A return of 0.5% to 2.9% per year for ten years isn't great. Once we consider the impact of inflation, things get worse. At the historical inflation level of roughly 3%, investors are likely to grow their wealth at between -2.5% and -0.1% per year for ten years.

Yikes.

That's trouble for investors accumulating wealth, but it's especially troubling for retirees — who are actively taking money out of their portfolios to pay bills. At the industry recommended 4% withdrawal rate, it's entirely possible that if you are retired or will retire soon — your real investment value (after inflation) will decrease by 4% to 6.5% per year for ten years.

Assuming you've got another 30 years to live — that could be some severe damage to your nest egg.

I don't want that fate for you. By adopting the Dividend Growth Investing mindset, I think you can significantly improve on the returns most of your friends, family, and neighbors will get on their balanced mutual funds.

Dividend Growth Investing: The Boring, Predictable Path to Wealth

The strategy I will outline in this book is not the most exciting. There are no complicated math formulas to follow. In fact, anyone that got beyond junior high school has already conquered the complexity needed to follow it. There are no revolutionary stock-picking techniques here. It's not a "get rich quick" method. You won't see any TV ads about it.

You don't need a Ph.D. in finance or a fancy MBA from Harvard. In fact, those things might get in your way. After all, Wall Street tends to take simple things and make them complicated.

What the strategy lacks in excitement, it makes up for in practical application and results. This strategy works if you apply it over many years. Slowly, but surely – this strategy will grow your wealth consistently and predictably over time.

If you're looking for investments that will double overnight, this book isn't for you. It's not about picking the next Facebook, Amazon, Google, or Netflix.

This book is about investing in real companies that make real money. It's about focusing on long-term results rather than short-term price changes. Unlike most of Wall Street's gibberish, this strategy is simple, logical, and easy-to-understand. It's the most boring, predictable way to build wealth investing in common stocks.

It's better than savings accounts, hiding cash under the mattress, bonds, and annuities. It's a way to safely withdraw money throughout retirement to ensure that you never run out.

If that sounds good to you, then I hope you will join me. You've already endured 5 minutes. Only 68 to go!

1871 through 2016, the stock market produces a compounded return of 9.07% per year. That's enough to grow \$1 into \$319,492. No typos.

Yet, few understand how they can profit from it. Even fewer will accomplish investing success. In the words of Warren Buffet, "Investing is simple, but not easy."

The strategy I will outline in this book is not the most exciting. There are no complicated math formulas to follow or any revolutionary stock-picking techniques. It's not a "get rich quick" method. You won't see any TV ads about it.

However, it works. Slowly, but surely, this strategy will grow your wealth consistently and predictably over time.

This book is about investing in real companies that make real money. It's about focusing on long-term results rather than short-term price changes. Unlike most of Wall Street's gibberish, this strategy is simple, logical, and easy-to-understand. It's the most boring, predictable way to build wealth investing in common stocks.

It's better than savings accounts, hiding cash under the mattress, bonds, and annuities. It's a way to safely withdraw money throughout retirement to ensure that you never run out.

If that sounds good to you, then I hope you will join me for the next 47 minutes. I want to introduce you to dividend growth investing. It's the most powerful investment strategy you'll find.

PART ONE
DIVIDENDS &
RETIREMENT

In the first part of the book, we'll explore how dividend growth investing compares to traditional solutions for retirement.

In Chapter 1, we'll see how Mr. Market causes problems for our hypothetical retired couple — Jim & Sally. We'll also see if they can make it on a 100% bond portfolio. And then we'll see what an annuity can do for them.

In Chapter 2, we'll see how Jim & Sally do with a traditional "balanced" portfolio that decreases stocks as they age.

In Chapter 3, we'll dream up what the "perfect" retirement strategy would do and see if dividend growth investing checks all the boxes.

1

RETIREMENT
& MR. MARKET

"Mr. Market's job is to provide you with prices; your job is to decide whether it is to your advantage to act on them. You do not have to trade with him just because he constantly begs you to." -Benjamin Graham

One day, you're going to get tired of working. However, your bills aren't going to get tired of being paid. So how do you make money when you aren't working?

Most people will work 40 years to build up a nest egg. Once they retire, they start taking money out of their accounts to pay bills. The question becomes: "How much can I spend each year and not run out of money?"

Most investment advisors recommend that you sell 4% of your nest egg each year to fund expenses and increase that withdrawal rate over time to keep up with inflation. Let's follow a hypothetical couple named Jim and Sally to illustrate how it works.

The Typical Retirement Plan

Jim and Sally have worked their entire lives. They are now ready to kick back, relax, and enjoy time with their kids and grandkids. They have saved up for years and have built up a $500,000 portfolio. Both turned 62 this year and will soon be collecting $3,000 per month in Social Security benefits.

Jim and Sally spend $50,000 per year. Social Security covers more than half of their spending, but they are still $20,000 short. Without a paycheck, their investment accounts will have to cover the difference. Jim and Sally meet with a financial advisor to discuss their options. He tells them stocks return an average of 9% per year, so that's what they can expect in the future.

He tells them they can take out 4% of their account value ($20,000) each year and never run out of money. A 9% return on a $500,000 account would be $45,000 per year. As long as they take out $20,000 per year, they will have $25,000 left over to re-invest into their account. Over time, their account will grow, and they'll be able to take even more out.

In theory, this makes a lot of sense. As long as their portfolio grows by 9% each year, Jim and Sally have nothing to worry about. Unfortunately, Jim and Sally haven't met Mr. Market.

Who Is Mr. Market?

Legendary investor Ben Graham introduces Mr. Market in his book "The Intelligent Investor." Mr. Market is the person on the other end of your stock market trades. Mr. Market wants to buy your shares of stock. Every day, he quotes you a price at which he will buy your shares of stock or sell you some of his.

The problem is Mr. Market is a manic depressive. When he is in a good mood, Mr. Market is willing to pay you high prices for your stocks. When he is in a foul mood, he doesn't offer much for your shares.

His mood fluctuates wildly from day-to-day, week-to-week, and month-to-month. Mr. Market might be willing to pay you $40 for shares of Coca-Cola on Monday and $45 on Tuesday. A few months later, he might not even pay $25 for your shares.

You don't have to take Mr. Market up on his offers, but he will always quote you a price.

Every. Single. Day.

It's easy to ignore Mr. Market's price quotes when you are buying shares. As Jim and Sally added to their investments, they bought from Mr. Market whether prices went up or down.

Things get more difficult when you start relying on Mr. Market's mood swings to pay your bills. Jim and Sally now have to start selling $20,000 worth of their stocks back to Mr. Market each year. If Mr. Market has a bad day, they will have to take him up on his offer to buy their shares - even if it's at a low price.

Let's see how the 4% strategy works out for them using actual market returns from 1999 through 2015.

Year #1

In the first year of their retirement, Jim and Sally run into a bad year in the market. Their mutual funds are down by -9%.

After taking out $20,000 to pay expenses, Jim and Sally's portfolio has dropped below $435,000. Jim is particularly concerned and asks their advisor if they've made a mistake. Will he have to go back to work?

Their advisor assures them that markets go up and down. This down period is a speed bump. Stock prices will come back up over time.

Year #2

Mr. Market continues to be in a foul mood in Year #2. Jim and Sally's accounts are down another -11.8% (or minus $51,000). On top of that, they took out another $20,000 to pay bills. Their account balance at the end of the year falls below $363,000.

Was investing in stocks the right thing to do? Should they even be in the market at all? Their advisor assures them that the market will come back. "Hold tight," he tells them.

To be safe, their advisor recommends they reduce withdrawals from $20,000 to $14,500 per year. Unfortunately, Jim and Sally can't do that. Sally has to have surgery this spring, so they will need the entire $20,000.

Year #3

Unfortunately, Mr. Market's bad mood continues into the 3rd year. The market is down by -22%, and Jim and Sally's portfolio continues to plummet. By the end of the 3rd year, Jim and Sally's account is worth $261,813 - down nearly 50% from when they started.

Jim and Sally are terrified. They thought their nest egg would get them through retirement. Mr. Market had other ideas. Instead of living a comfortable retirement, Jim and Sally might have to go back to work.

What Now?

Most people cannot watch their nest egg fall by 50% and remain committed to their original plan. The emotional toll is too enormous. Jim and Sally go to their advisor and demand that he sell their shares and move to cash. Jim and Sally lock in their severe losses and miss out on the future stock market recovery. As a result, they end up running out of money in ten years.

If Jim and Sally had kept with their investment plan, their money would have lasted much longer.

The next chart shows their account value if they continued to invest in stocks. Unfortunately, the damage to their account was done. Jim and Sally would have still run out of money by age 86.[1]

Jim and Sally would invest a little differently if they had a 2nd chance. They might have chosen something safer than the stock market and moody Mr. Market.

Why Not Stick with "Safe" Bonds?

If they could go back in time, Jim and Sally might explain to their investment advisor that stocks are too risky. "Why should we own stocks at all? They are too volatile," Jim declares. "We need something safe!" Their advisor recommends investing in a portfolio of 100% bonds.

---

[1] This assumes the same market returns as the S&P 500 from 1999-2015 followed by 8% per year from age 76 onward. Also assumes Jim and Sally started taking out $20,000 per year at age 62 and increased that withdrawal at a constant rate of 3%. Source of market returns: New York University, January 2016. Past performance is not an indicator of future returns.

Their advisor explains that when you buy a bond, you lend money to a company or government. In exchange, the borrower agrees to pay you interest and pay you back one day. For example, a 10-year U.S. Treasury bond has an interest rate of 2.5%. If you bought $10,000 worth of this bond, you would collect $250 per year in interest. When the ten years are up, you get your $10,000 back.

Bonds are considered "safer" because you know what return you will get whenever you buy it. As long as the borrower can afford to pay you back, you'll always make a positive return. Mr. Market still quotes a new price every day, but he's not as manic depressive with bonds. His quote generally stays around the same value.

Jim and Sally's advisor finds them a bucket of corporate bonds paying 4% interest per year.[2] Perfect, right? With their $500,000 portfolio, those bonds will pay $20,000 per year in interest.

---

[2] As of December 2016, the Vanguard Intermediate-Term Corporate Bond ETF (VCIT) had an SEC yield of 3.4% per year. The Vanguard Long-Term Corporate Bond ETF had an SEC yield of 4.6% per year. A 50/50 portfolio would produce an average yield of 4% per year.

That is exactly what they need to cover their spending. Now they don't have to worry about the stock market! Since Jim and Sally no longer own stocks, Mr. Market's manic-depressive mood swings are of no concern to them. They love their advisor's new plan! A 100% bond portfolio is surely the way to go.

The Silent Killer of All Retirement Plans

Unfortunately, there is a problem with Jim and Sally's all-bond portfolio. It's called inflation.

Jim and Sally's expenses will continue to increase each year as the prices at the grocery store go up.

On average, inflation runs about 3%. So a $1 bill today will be able to purchase about $0.97 worth of groceries next year. Then $0.94 the year after that. Over the next 25 years, every dollar in your pocket will buy $0.50 worth of stuff. In other words, if your grocery bill is $400 per month today, it will be $800 in 25 years.

That means Jim and Sally have to keep taking more and more out of their account each year to keep up with rising costs. Jim and Sally are earning $20,000 per year in interest. Unfortunately, this income stays constant. Their portfolio may be producing $20,000 per year, but they end up taking more each year as their expenses grow.

While their spending goes up, their income does not. To make up for it, Jim and Sally have to start selling chunks of their bonds to pay their bills. The next chart shows what happens.

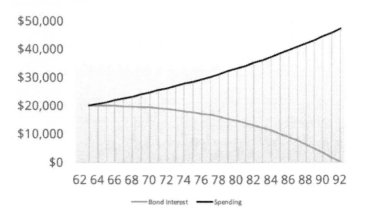

Their expenses (black line) increase faster than the bond interest produced (gray line).

Jim and Sally have to sell a few bonds each year to cover the difference. This does severe damage to their account because the bonds they sold don't pay interest. So next year, they will earn less than $20,000 in interest, and they will need to take out even more than $20,000.

The destruction of their portfolio snowballs over time. They need to sell more bonds to cover more expenses. The more bonds they sell, however, the less interest is there in the next year.

That's not good.

Jim and Sally will eventually run out of bonds to sell. As their bonds get sold, the interest payments go away. The cycle repeats itself until Jim and Sally either run out of money or have to lower their spending.

What about Annuities?

Fortunately, Jim and Sally still have their time machine. They would go back in time and tell their advisor that stocks are too risky and bonds don't keep up with inflation.

They ask him, "What else is there?" He tells them about a financial product called an "annuity." The advisor likes annuities because he makes a huge commission from them. For every annuity he sells, their advisor can make 4% to 7% up front. If he sells an "equity-indexed annuity," he can make 5% to 12%[3]! What a deal – for the advisor that is!

The annuity is an easy sale. Jim and Sally's advisor tells them that the payments are "guaranteed" income for life. If the stock market goes down, your account won't go down with it. What a great solution!

Unfortunately, annuities don't solve any of Jim and Sally's problems. In fact, they make things worse. Here's why.

Annuities have the same problem that bonds have – their income is fixed.

---

[3] Lankford, Kimberly, "The Great Annuity Rip-Off." Kiplinger, December 2007.

While the cost of groceries is going up, your annuity check is the same year-after-year. Some insurance policies come with "inflation riders" that increase payments with inflation. Unfortunately, you pay for the inflation protection by taking lower initial payments.

When you buy an annuity, that money is gone.

People are afraid of stocks because they don't want their $500,000 to fall to $250,000. So they buy annuities to "protect themselves against market declines."

That's ironic. When you buy an annuity, your $500,000 goes to $0. Z-E-R-O. All that money goes to the insurance company. You still get the payments, but your original principal is gone.

Do you know what happens with that $500,000 check Jim and Sally mailed to the insurance company? The insurance company invests it in stocks and bonds. So you were afraid to invest the $500,000 in the markets, so you paid the insurance company to do it for you. Why not save the high fees and commission checks and invest it yourself?

Annuity income is "guaranteed," but that may not be as great as it sounds. If the insurance company goes out of business, what do you think happens to your annuity checks?

If there is no insurance company left to pay your annuity payments, they go away. That $500,000 vanishes into thin air.

If you're thinking about buying an annuity, make sure you understand all the terms first. Also, make sure you know how much your so-called "advisor" is going to make on them. In most cases, the fees, commissions, and the 2,000-page document should be enough to steer you away.

2

THE AGE-BASED "SOLUTION"

"When it is obvious that the goals cannot be reached, don't adjust the goals, adjust the action steps." —*Confucius*

In the last chapter, we saw that Jim and Sally faced two enemies threatening their retirement:

Mr. Market

Jim and Sally planned to live off of the price increases of their stocks, but that didn't work out. Mr. Market was in a bad mood, and they had to sell him some of their stock at low prices to pay the bills.

Inflation

Jim and Sally's expenses increased each year. The income from their bond portfolio didn't. Neither did the annuity income.

These are the two problems facing all retirees and future retirees. Finance academics have proposed a solution. Own a diversified portfolio of a bunch of different assets.

The academics tell you a portfolio of 100% stocks is too risky. It makes you vulnerable to Mr. Market's mood swings. A portfolio of 100% bonds is also too risky. You risk of falling behind inflation. Their solution is to own some of both.

The question then becomes: How much of both?

Age-Based Investing

Academics tell us that a 20-year-old should invest in more stocks than a 60-year-old. This makes sense. The younger person has 40 years to recover from a bad spell in the stock market. The younger you are, the more of your portfolio should be in stocks. The older you get, the more you shift your portfolio to bonds. Simple, right?

Most advisors tell you to start with 100 and subtract your age. That is the percentage you should invest in stocks with the rest going into bonds.

For example, a 30-year-old would own 70% stocks and 30% bonds. An 80-year-old would have 20% in stocks and 80% bonds.

An older person can't afford for their portfolio to decline in value by 50%. To help mitigate the risk of stocks, they should put a larger percentage in bonds.

For a long time, this has been the conventional wisdom on Wall Street. However, today's retiree's may need more money in stocks to keep up with inflation and preserve their spending power.

No kidding. With retirement lasting longer than it ever has before and interest rates at all-time lows, retirees following the age-based model may be in trouble.

The Age-Based Model Makes No Sense

Let's say a woman walks into a car dealership. She doesn't know much about cars, so she finds a sales manager and asks him if he can make a recommendation for her.

The sales manager asks her how old she is. She tells him that she is 30 years old. "OK," he says, "I know just the car for you." He walks her over to the minivan section and recommends a 2015 Toyota Sienna.

Just because the woman is at the right age to be married with kids doesn't mean she needs a minivan. If you were making a car recommendation, don't you think you would want more information than a person's age?

You would want to know how many people would ride in the vehicle. You might need to know how they planned to use it. Many factors would influence your recommendation.

As significant as a car buy may be, it's not as important as your investment decisions. Even small changes to your investment returns make a big difference. Consider that $100,000 invested at 3% grows to $242,000 in 30 years. That same $100,000 invested at 9% grows to more than $1.3 million.

Age alone seems a bit inadequate for such a huge decision, don't you think? Yet the vast majority of so-called "experts" still rely on age as the primary variable. It's not.

Age Is Not the Only Variable

There are more factors to consider than age. What about:

- Other income sources (Social Security, pension, part-time job)
- Future cash flow needs
- Expected retirement age

- Reliability of income
- Major one-time expenses or contributions
- Changes in lifestyle
- Risk preferences

Few Can Stick with 100% Stocks Long-Term

Let's say you invested $100,000 into the S&P 500 in January 2007 then slipped into a coma for ten years. When you woke up, you would have been delighted to see your money at $195,000.

If you had remained conscious, you would have watched your account value cut in half by May of 2009 . Would you have been able to watch your account fall by 50% and still held on? Or would you have panicked and sold at the bottom?

Many people weren't able to weather the 2008-09 recession. The same people that were telling their friends to "buy low and sell high" ended up doing the exact opposite. They sold when the market was down by 53%. Now that the S&P 500 index has recovered by 250%+ . they still haven't bought back into stocks.

Investing is more about your emotions than your brains. If you can't stomach major declines in stock prices, you either need a new strategy or an advisor. If you decide to hire someone to help, I'll give you some tips in a few chapters.

Lower Volatility Usually Comes with Lower Returns

Stocks will almost always outperform bonds over long periods of time (think 15+ years). If you have a long time horizon, bonds will likely reduce your returns.

At the time of writing, you could buy a 30-year US Treasury bond and earn 3.0% per year[4]. A 100% stock portfolio will run circles around bonds over the next 30 years. Going back to 1928, stocks have never produced less than 7% over any 30-year period. However, let's assume that stocks produce even less than that – just 6% per year.

The difference between 3% and 6% is unbelievable. A 3% return would turn your $100,000 investment into $242,726. At 6%, that same investment grows to $574,349.

That's even assuming that stocks return less than they have over any 30-year period! If the past is anything like the future, stocks will likely outperform bonds by even more than that. Investing in bonds comes with less volatility, but also lowers your expected returns.

Bottom line: The "asset allocation" strategy is all about trade-offs. As a result, it ends up being an OK solution with lukewarm results. There has to be a better way.

---

[4] Source: US Federal Reserve

3

THE PERFECT
RETIREMENT STRATEGY

"Do you know the only thing that gives me pleasure? It's to see my dividends come in." –John D. Rockefeller

So far, we've seen how different investment strategies fall short in one way or another. Let's imagine for a moment that we could design the perfect investment. What would it look like?

The perfect investment strategy should do five things:

1. It should grow our wealth reliably over long periods of time (15+ years).
2. It should minimize the volatility of our portfolio so we can sleep well at night.
3. It should generate reliable income to pay our bills.

4. That income should grow at least as fast as our expenses.

5. It should be easy-to-understand and follow.

There is only one strategy I know of that can do all five things: dividend growth investing. Let's see if it can check all the boxes.

Provide High Enough Returns to Build Real Wealth

If you would have invested $100,000 in dividend growth stocks in 1972, it would have grown to nearly $6,000,000 by 2015[5]. It would have even outperformed the S&P 500 index over that time frame – something most mutual funds fail to do.

Does it provide high returns for building wealth? Check.

---

[5] Assuming you would have invested in "Dividend Growers and Initiators" basket of stocks starting in 1972 and re-investing all dividends through 2015. Source: Ned Davis Research.

Less Volatility than the Overall Stock Market

This strategy is far less risky (as measured by price volatility) than investing in an S&P 500 index fund. In 2008, the S&P 500 index fell by 37%[6]. A basket of dividend growth companies would have been down by almost half as much[7].

A portfolio of S&P 500 index funds would have had to own 30% bonds to reduce risk by that much[8]. Is it less volatile than the overall stock market? Check.

---

[6] Using the SPDR S&P 500 Index ETF (SPY) Source: Morningstar.

[7] Assuming an investment in the US Dividend Achievers Index (Used Vanguard's US Dividend Appreciation ETF "VIG" as a proxy). Source: Morningstar.

[8] Using the iShares US Barclays Bond Index ETF (AGG). A portfolio of 70% S&P 500 index and 30% AGG would have resulted in a similar return during 2008 as the Dividend Achievers Index ETF (VIG). Source: Morningstar.

Provide Reliable Cash Income

A $1 million investment in dividend stocks yielding 3% would produce more than $30,000 per year. That income does not depend on Mr. Market. The cash gets paid every year.

Does it provide reliable cash income? Check.

Grow that Income Faster than Inflation

That $30,000 per year in income will continue to grow faster than inflation each year. Assuming 6% dividend growth, that $30,000 income will increase to more than $172,000 in 30 years. And that's income only – not market value.

Does the income grow faster than inflation? Check.

Be Simple to Understand

Have you ever read an annuity contract? No. Of course, you haven't. No one has (not even the people selling them). Someone with a Ph.D. in aeronautics couldn't understand it. Most investment products are difficult to comprehend. There are many moving parts, formulas, calculations that make it hard to know what's going on with your money.

Even mutual funds or exchange-traded funds ("ETFs") can be difficult to understand. In these products, you are not the direct owner of the underlying stocks. You merely own the vehicle that owns the stock. Make sense? No? Ok. Bottom line: Most fund investors have no idea what they are invested in.

With a dividend growth strategy, you always know what you own. You can see the companies right on your account statement. It says "Coca-Cola" and "Apple" rather than "American Funds Growth Fund of America A shares." There is no middleman. Everything is right there for you to see.

Is it simple to understand? Check.

Over the next few chapters, I want to introduce you to dividend growth investing. Before we get too far, we need to cover the basics of what a dividend is and where they come from. To illustrate, let's follow a young man named Johnny as he finds some investors for his lemonade stand.

If you already are well versed in the basics of dividend policy, feel free to skip on to the next chapter. If you don't know much about dividends or where they come from, the next chapter is for you.

PART TWO
THE POWER OF
DIVIDENDS

In the second part of the book, we'll get into the mechanics of dividend investing.

Chapter 4 will be an introduction to the basics of dividend investing. We'll follow Johnny and his business — Johnny's Lemonade Stand — from a new company to an established dividend payer. We'll see the two ways investors make money in stocks — by dividends and capital gains. And we'll explore some basic valuation techniques. If you are an experienced investor — please feel free to skip this part!

In Chapter 5, we'll see how Dividend Growth — not Dividend Yield — is the engine that powers the Dividend Growth Investing strategy. Coca-Cola (KO) will be our real-life example of dividend growth in action.

In Chapter 6, we'll see how Dividend Reinvestment can power amazing increases in your wealth — even if the stock price goes down. This is a chapter geared towards those still building their assets — not necessarily retirees.

Chapter 7 will be about the historical track record of dividends compared to a passive strategy of buying the S&P 500 index.

And, finally, Chapter 8 will wrap up the section with a brief summary of reasons you might consider adding dividend investing to your investing arsenal.

4

JOHNNY & THE
LEMONADE STAND

"The prime purpose of a business corporation is to pay dividends regularly and, presumably, to increase the rate as time goes on." –Benjamin Graham

Johnny is an enterprising young man that would like to start earning some money. He decides that he wants to launch a lemonade business. He needs $200 to build a stand and buy a one-month supply of lemons and sugar.

The problem? His penny bank is empty.

To raise the money required for his business, Johnny has two options. He can either borrow the money or sell ownership in his business.

Which should he choose?

Option #1: He Could Borrow the Cash

Johnny could ask his neighborhood friends Jim and Tim to lend money to his business. Of course, they wouldn't do this for free. If Jim and Tim both gave Johnny $100 each, they would expect that he would pay them back in a few years with some interest.

In this scenario, Jim and Tim would buy a "bond" from Johnny's business. Jim and Tim will get their original money back plus interest as long as Johnny's company stays in business long enough to repay.

Option #2: He Could Sell Ownership in the Business

Johnny could also go to Jim and Tim and offer to sell them an ownership stake in his business. Under this arrangement, Jim and Tim would buy shares of stock in Johnny's business for $100 each.

Johnny's Lemonade Stand wouldn't have to pay this $100 back like it did in the bond scenario. If Jim and Tim owned stock, they would get a part of all future profits. If the company flourishes, Jim and Tim can make a lot of money. If it fails, they will be out their $100.

How Does a Stock Make Money for You?

A stock represents part ownership in a real business. But how does this "stock" make money for you? And where does that money come from?

Let's say Johnny decides to sell stock to fund his new lemonade stand. He divides the ownership stake into four pieces and sells one of those pieces each to Tim and one to Jim.

Since there are four shares, each share is worth 25% of the business. The current ownership structure of Johnny's Lemonade Stand is:

- Jim owns one share, which represents 25% of the business.
- Tim also owns one share for 25%.

- Johnny owns two shares or 50%.

There would be thousands, millions, even billions of these shares in a publicly traded company. For example, Apple currently has 5,472,800,000 shares outstanding. If you bought one of these shares, you would own 0.0000000001827218% of Apple's business.

If you had $617 billion, you could buy the whole company[9]. We'll work on getting you there.

For now, let's get back to Johnny and see what happens at his lemonade business over the next few years.

Year #1

In the first year, Johnny uses the investors' $200 to build his lemonade stand and buy lemons and sugar.

Johnny sets up shop, makes some delicious lemonade, and ends up selling $200 worth of it.

---

[9] Market cap as of September 2016. Source: Google Finance.

Johnny had $200 in sales but also $200 in expenses. So year #1 was a $0 profit. It wasn't a total failure, though. He developed a small customer base that he expects will grow next year.

Year #2

In the second year, Johnny's lemonade becomes more popular. His sales increase 5x to $1,000. His raw materials (sugar/lemon) expenses also increase to match the growing demand. After paying expenses, Johnny nets a profit of $200.

Johnny's business checking account now has $200 in it. He has a decision to make. What should he do with the $200 profit?

Johnny has two options. He can either (1) re-invest that money back into the business or (2) pay it out to his shareholders as a "dividend."

As much as he would like to have the money, Johnny thinks he could earn a higher return on it if he expanded the business. Johnny decides not to pay a dividend in year #2. Instead, he re-invests the $200 back into the company to build a second lemonade stand across town.

Year #3

In the third year, Johnny's second location doubles his sales to $2,000. Since Johnny is selling more lemonade, he's also buying more supplies. So he strikes a deal with a local grocery store to sell him lemons and sugar in bulk for a 10% discount.

This decrease in the cost of his raw materials allows Johnny to earn even more profit per cup. In the third year of operations, Johnny's stand earns $400.

Once again, Johnny faces a decision. The business has $400 that he needs to do something with. Should he pay it out to shareholders as a dividend or expand the business?

If Johnny were to pay the entire amount to shareholders, he would have nothing left to buy more lemons and sugar. So he decides to keep $200 in the business checking account and pay $200 out to shareholders as a dividend.

Way #1 Stocks Make You Money: Dividends

This brings us to the first way a stock makes money for you: dividend payments.

The $200 dividend payment gets paid to each shareholder based on how much of the business they own.

Since there are four shares, the $200 dividend gets split four ways. Johnny's Lemonade Stand pays out $50 to each share:

- Since Jim owns one share, he gets $50.
- Tim also gets $50 for his share.
- Johnny owns two shares, so he gets $50 x 2 = $100.

Johnny's Lemonade Stand transfers the appropriate amount to each shareholders' bank account.

The dividend works the same way in a publicly traded company, just on a much larger scale. For example, Apple paid $12,022,000,000 out to their shareholders over the past year[10]. If you owned the entire company, you would have received more than $12 billion in dividends.

But no one person owns all of Apple. That massive $12 billion payout was split amongst the 5.4 billion shares. If you owned one share, you would have received $2.16 in the last year. If you owned ten shares, you would have received $21.60. And 100 shares would bring you $216 in dividends. The more shares you own, the higher your dividend payout will be.

Dividends are the most reliable way that stocks make you money. As long as the business continues to earn positive profits, you will get a part of that paid out to you in cash.

---

[10] Source: Apple 2015 10-K report.

The second way stocks make money for you is price appreciation. We'll talk about that next.

Way #2 Stocks Make You Money: Price Growth

Most people don't think much about dividends when it comes to investing in stocks. Getting a $2 payout from Apple each year is boring. Think about it. Have you ever seen a New York Times headline that said: "Apple Pays $2.16 in Dividends!" No. That's not going to get anyone to read the newspaper.

People read newspapers with headlines: "Dow Crashes 500 Points in Single Day!" or "Double Your Money in 2 Months with These 10 Stocks!"

It is far more exciting to buy Apple at $100 and hope its stock price goes up to $200! Stock price changes are where the real action is on Wall Street and is what 99.9% of people talk about.

These changes happen every day. Sometimes stocks go up, and sometimes they go down. Over the long run, they will likely go up.

But why is that? Why do stocks tend to increase in price over long periods of time? What is the real driver of that value? Let's check back in with Johnny and his lemonade stand to find out.

Let's say ten years have gone by since Jim and Tim made their investment. Johnny's Lemonade Stand has continued to increase its profits year-after-year. The business now has lemonade stands in several major cities and unique 10 locations. Johnny partnered with several restaurants in these cities that sell lemonade to customers. In the most recent year, Johnny sold $5,000 worth of lemonade and earned profits of $1,000.

Now let's assume that one of the investors decides he would like to sell his shares. Tim approaches Mike from across town. How much do you think Mike will offer to pay Tim for his shares? That depends on several different factors:

How Much Could Mike Earn on Other Investments?

Johnny's Lemonade Stand isn't Mike's only investment opportunity. He could buy real estate, invest in bonds, purchase stock in a different business, or stash money away in his savings account at the local bank.

To make it simple, let's assume Mike has two choices: earn 10% in his checking account or invest in Johnny's Lemonade Stand.

Do you think Mike would be willing to invest in Johnny's Lemonade stand if he expected to make 10%? No way!

Why? The bank account is a sure bet. Johnny's Lemonade Stand is far from it. There are a lot of things that could go wrong with Johnny's stand. Competitors could come in with a better recipe and ruin the company's sales. Customers could develop a taste for an alternative product like iced tea.

Why would Mike take more risk to earn the same 10% return? He wouldn't. He will either put his money in the bank or pay a lower price for a share of Lemonade Stand stock.

Now let's assume the bank stops offering 10% and starts offering 1%. Now Johnny's Lemonade Stand looks a lot more attractive. A 10% return on the stock would be dramatically better than what Mike could get at the bank, so he's a much more willing buyer.

Interest rates influence stock prices because they set the minimum level that investors require on all other risky investments. Higher interest rates make bank deposits, bonds, and other fixed-income securities more attractive.

What is the Future Growth of Profits?

Would you prefer to own a company with increasing profits or decreasing profits? Of course, you want to buy a business that will grow in the future.

Mike will be willing to pay more for a share of Johnny's Lemonade Stand if he believes its profits will grow. Without business growth, companies are worth far less. We will explore this later in the chapter.

What is the Company's Financial Health?

Would you lend money to a friend that had $100,000 in debt and no job? Of course not! Why? You won't get your money back. In the same way, Mike will be less attracted to Johnny's Lemonade Stand if the company has a lot of debt.

Putting It All Together: What Will Mike Pay?

Let's follow Mike's thought process as he decides what price to offer Tim for his share.

Mike thinks Johnny's stand can continue to make $1,000 per year for the foreseeable future. He also expects the company will continue to pay at least $125 in dividends for each share.

Mike can earn 5% in his bank account, so he wants to be sure he can earn at least 5%. Preferably, he would like to make a lot more considering how risky the business could be. Mike decides a 10% return would be acceptable for him.

To calculate what he would be willing to pay per share, Mike takes his $125 dividend and divides that by 10%. That gives him a fair price of $1,250 for one share of Johnny's Lemonade Stand.

If he were to make this investment, he would get paid $125 per year. That would be a 10% return on his initial investment of $1,250.

Simple enough, right? Now, let's throw another wrench into the equation: growth.

Dividend Growth: The Key to Value

If Mike expects Johnny's Lemonade Stand to continue to grow its profits and dividends each year, he will be willing to pay far more for the share than $1,250.

Let's assume Mike believes Johnny's stand will grow its profits by 6% each year. That would result in Mike's $125 dividend payout growing to $132 in year #2, $140 in year #3, and so on.

To evaluate the shares, Mike will use a simple formula:

Starting Dividend per Share / Price per Share = Desired Annual Return – Expected Dividend Growth

If we plug in everything Mike knows about the Lemonade Stand, he will come up with:

$125 (initial dividend) / Price per Share (what he's trying to find) = 10% (desired return) - 6% (growth).

After working out the math, Mike would come up with a price of $3,125. That is what he should pay for the shares if he wants to get a 10% rate of return.

If you aren't completely following the math, don't worry about it. But do grab the concept here. Investors are willing to pay a higher price for a stock with future dividend growth.

In this example, Mike paid a hefty premium for the promise of future dividend growth. Without any growth, Mike was only willing to pay $1,250 for a share of Johnny's Lemonade Stand. With 6% growth, Mike was willing to pay $3,125.

Why is dividend growth worth so much? We'll find out in the next chapter!

5

THE POWER OF DIVIDEND GROWTH

"The very attention we place on rising dividends puts us squarely in the position of 'owners' of a company, of true investors who understand that a satisfying and reasonable return from a stock investment isn't a gift of the market or luck or the consequence of listening to some market maven, but it is the logical and inevitable result of investing in a company that is actually doing well enough, in the real world, to both pay dividends and to increase them on a regular basis." –Lowell Miller

Now you understand the basic mechanics of how an investment makes you money. Now let's get into the specifics about dividend growth investing and why it's such a powerful strategy.

Coca-Cola: A Real Example

Let's assume you have $1,000 to invest today, and you decide to buy shares of high-quality dividend company Coca-Cola (ticker symbol "KO").

You know what Coca-Cola does, right? They make sugary soda water with lots of chemicals in it (aka "Coca-Cola"). You might have heard of it. If you're one of those organic, sugar-free types – you're still funding Coca-Cola's profits. They also make Dasani water, Simply Orange, Vitaminwater, Smartwater, Fuze, and Honest Tea.

Coca-Cola makes a lot of stuff. But most of all, they make money. And a lot of it. Coca-Cola made $7.6 billion of profit in 2015. Of which, they paid out $5.9 billion.[11] Dividends aren't anything new to the company. They have paid and increased their dividend for 53 consecutive years. If you aren't excited about that yet, you will be.

---

[11] Source: Coca-Cola (KO) 2015 10-K report.

Back to you and your $1,000 investment. Coca-Cola currently trades for about $40 per share. That means your $1,000 would be enough to buy 25 shares. You now own a part owner (a very small one) in Coca-Cola's business. Congratulations!

Now, the fun part begins.

Coca-Cola's current dividend is $0.33 per share[12]. Since you own 25 shares, you'll get $8.25 paid to your bank account every three months.

So your first year of owning Coca-Cola will produce about $33 in dividends. You made a return of 3.3% in year #1 as a percent of your initial investment.

I know, I know. You're not impressed. Keep reading.

Remember that Coca-Cola has not only paid a dividend for 53 consecutive years. They've also increased it for 53 years. That's a big difference.

---

[12] Source: Google Finance, September 2016.

Let's assume Coca-Cola keeps selling sugar water in the future. They keep making more money and continue raising their dividend for the next 20 years. By how much? They've grown it by 8.5% per year over the past ten years, so we'll estimate 6% per year[13].

The next chart shows how your dividend payments would grow over time.

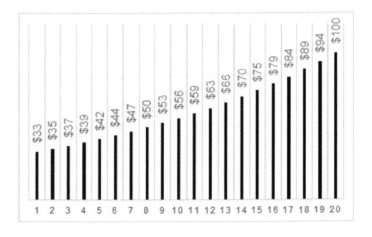

---

[13] Calculated using a 10-year CAGR from 2005 to 2015. Data source: Morningstar.

By year #20, you would be collecting $99 per year in dividend income - triple your original amount! If you add all 20 years of dividend payments together, it would add up to $1,214. That's even more than your initial investment!

Do you see what that means? If you buy shares of a company that pays a starting dividend yield of 3.3% and the dividend grows by 6% per year, you can't lose money. The dividend income alone exceeded your original $1,000 investment. Even if Coca-Cola's stock price dropped from $40 to $0, you would not lose a dime.

Dividend payments get paid to you regardless of what happens to the market value of your shares. I can't stress that enough: dividends get paid regardless of what happens to stock prices.

Coca-Cola's stock price could fluctuate from today's price of $40 down to $30. Most investors (and Wall Street gurus) would freak out. The market value was $1,000 and is now just $750! Panic! Sell, sell, sell!

Then the stock goes up to $50. Buy, buy, buy! Then back down to $35, and the panic starts all over again...

As a dividend investor, you don't care about Coca-Cola's stock price. It doesn't matter. That $0.33 dividend is still coming in three months. And 3 months from then. And three months from then...

Let's see what would happen to Coca-Cola's stock price under various different price scenarios.

What Would Happen to Coca-Cola's Stock Price?

Back to you and your 25 shares of Coca-Cola.

Coca-Cola's dividend continues to grow by 6% per year. Remember your measly $0.33 per share in dividend income? Yeah, that's going to be a lot higher. After 20 years, Coca-Cola's dividend per share would have increased from $1.32 to $4.00 per year.

What would the stock price be in 20 years? We can't know for sure. However, we can know it will likely be much higher than the $40 per share that you bought it for.

To prove that out, let's assume for a second that Coca-Cola's stock price stays at $40 for 20 years in a row. In 20 years, Coca-Cola would be paying $4 per share. That means another investor could buy and make 10% per year from dividends alone.

But don't forget about the $4 dividend.

Other people would see that 10% yield and start to drool. A virtual guaranteed 10% return in one of the best companies on Earth is a great investment! Investors would fall all over themselves trying to buy some shares.

All the buying would push the price of Coca-Cola's stock higher. How high? We don't know for sure. We do know that Coca-Cola's price will go up enough that the $4 dividend is a more reasonable initial return. A quality company should never have a dividend yield of 10%. It is an obvious buy at that level.

So what should the dividend yield be to make it more reasonable?

The following table shows what Coca-Cola's $4 dividend looks like at various prices.

Dividend		Price		Yield
$4.00	/	$40	=	10.0%
$4.00	/	$42	=	9.5%
$4.00	/	$44	=	9.1%
$4.00	/	$47	=	8.5%
$4.00	/	$50	=	8.0%
$4.00	/	$53	=	7.5%
$4.00	/	$57	=	7.0%
$4.00	/	$62	=	6.5%
$4.00	/	$67	=	6.0%
$4.00	/	$73	=	5.5%
$4.00	/	$80	=	5.0%
$4.00	/	$89	=	4.5%
$4.00	/	$100	=	4.0%
$4.00	/	$114	=	3.5%
$4.00	/	$133	=	3.0%

Which of these initial yields is low enough that other investors would stop drooling? To answer that question, we can look back at history to see what Coca-Cola's yield has been in years past.

In March 2009, Coca-Cola paid $0.84 per share in dividends. You could buy a share for $22, which made the initial yield 3.8%[14]. That's about as high as it has been for KO in quite some time.

In May of 2013, Coca-Cola's initial yield got as low as 2.5%[15].

If we use that as our guide, we conclude that Coca-Cola's initial yield is likely to stay somewhere between 2.5% and 4%.

If it pays a $4 dividend in 20 years, we can calculate its estimated stock price. We divide the dividend ($4) by estimated yield. At a 4% yield, the stock price in 20 years would be $100. At a 2.5% yield, the stock price would be $160[16]!

---

[14] Calculated using data from Google Finance.

[15] Source: Dividend.com.

[16] This assumes you take the $4 dividend and divide by the "worst case" yield of 4%. $4/0.04 = $100. For the "best case" yield, you would take the same $4 dividend and divide by 0.025 = $160. Of course, the past is not an indicator of the future

Do you see what's happening here? As Coca-Cola's dividend grows, its stock price is moving with it. The dividend acts like gravity. The stock price can go down in the short-term, but it can't go down forever. The dividend payment becomes too enticing and the stock's price must rise to keep pace.

This is a key point: A growing dividend puts upward pressure on a stock's price. Over a long enough period, it's impossible for the price not to grow with the dividend.

You are starting to see the power of dividends. There still something we haven't considered: dividend re-investment.

6

YOUR SECRET WEAPON: DIVIDEND REINVESTMENT

"A stock dividend is something tangible — it's not an earnings projection; it's something solid, in hand. A stock dividend is a true return on the investment. Everything else is hope and speculation." –Richard Russell

It should be evident by now how appealing dividend growth investing is for retired people. They need their investments to produce income for them. And that income needs to grow over time to keep pace with inflation. Dividends are the perfect way to do that.

What if you are still working and adding to your portfolio? Are dividends relevant for you? Most people assume dividends are for retired folks only. That couldn't be further from the truth!

Those dividend payments have to go somewhere. If you aren't spending them on groceries, what will you spend the money on? Stocks, of course! Dividends are available to be re-invested back into more dividend paying stocks. The result is two forms of compounding: the dividends and the number of shares you own. As the number of shares you own increases, so does the future income. And the virtuous cycle compounds on top of itself until it can't be stopped.

Let's see how it works.

The Incredible Power of Re-Invested Dividends

I know you're tired of Coke now, but let's re-visit it one more time. Back to the beginning. Ok, you just bought your 25 shares of Coca-Cola's stock at $40. You get the same $33 worth of dividends in the first year.

In this case, you're not taking the $33 out to spend. You re-invest it back into Coca-Cola's stock. For lack of a more creative word, this is known as "dividend reinvestment."

How many additional shares would your $33 buy? Well, that depends on the stock price. If Coke's stock is trading for $100, you won't be able to buy as many new shares. And vice versa.

To keep it simple, let's say the price stays at $40. Your $33 dividend would buy an extra 0.83 shares. Here's where you start to make some hay.

In year #2, you have 25.83 shares. That's an increase of 3.3% over the prior year. And Coca-Cola is going to increase the dividend per share by 6%.

You increased your dividend income from $33 in year #1 to $36.14 in year #2. That's an increase of 9.5%.

Now you have $36.14 to do something with. Of course, you're not going to spend this money on anything but more shares of Coke at this point. Are you? Come on. You know you're not.

If the stock price stays at $40, your $36.14 can buy 0.90 more shares. That brings your total share count to 26.7 shares.

The same thing happens in Year #3. Your share count goes up as you re-invest your dividends. And the dividend goes up when the company increases it each year. As both increase, your dividend income grows. This allows you to buy even more shares. And the cycle goes on and on.

Over time, these reinvested shares start to add up and compound. The chart on the next page shows how those shares grow over time.

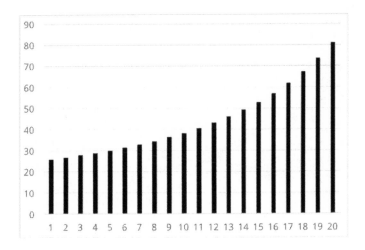

Fast forward to year #20. You have re-invested your dividends and now own 73 shares of Coca-Cola. Not only have you been growing your share count, but the dividend has been going up as well. That makes your dividend income go bonkers.

Just look at the chart on the next page.

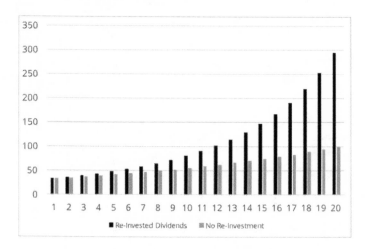

The gray line shows your dividend income if you don't re-invest the money. In other words, if you're a retired person and you take the money out. Or burn it. You know, whatever you want to do with it. The black line shows your dividend income if you re-invest your dividends. Amazing, right?

With the re-invested dividends, you would collect $2,238 in dividend income over 20 years. That is double your original investment of $1,000. And we haven't even gotten to price yet...

What Would My Rate of Return Be?

Coca-Cola's stock price hasn't budged from $40. So you don't make any money from price appreciation. Don't be too sad, though. You still would have made a fortune.

At $40 per share, your 73 shares would have a market value of $2,944 at the end of year #20[17]. Even though the stock price went flat for 20 years, you would have earned a $1,944 profit. That is almost triple your original investment!

Please don't miss what happened here. You invested in one of the most stable companies on Earth. They did not grow their dividend all that fast (6% isn't impressive). Not only that, but the stock price didn't go up a single dollar! Despite your "bad pick," you still made a 194% profit over a 20-year period.

---

[17] Assuming you were able to re-invest dividends at $40 per share, your initial 25 shares would grow to 73.6 at the end of Year #20. If you take those 73.6 shares multiplied by $40 per share, that would equal $2,944

That's the real genius of the dividend strategy. You don't have to be good at picking stocks. You don't even have to be average at it. You can be the worst stock picker on Earth and still make an impressive profit!

Yeah, this is exciting stuff.

Ok, so you doubters say, "But what if Coca-Cola's stock price crashes - won't I lose my money?"

Dear Wall Street: Please Skip This Section

WARNING: Do not repeat what you read in this section. Your friends will look at you like you've lost your mind. And they will think you have. But you haven't.

Here's the shocker: as a dividend investor, you would prefer that the stock market go down in value. Not up.

Please don't stop reading this book now. Let me explain.

We went through an example with Coca-Cola's stock staying at $40. Now let's assume its stock falls to $20 immediately after you buy it. And the stock price never recovers. Not even after 20 years.

Can you imagine the chaos this would cause on Wall Street? Account values halved with no hope for any positive returns. But you? You'd be jumping for joy. Here's why.

In year #1, you still receive your $33 in dividend income like you did in our previous example. Always remember, dividend income and stock prices are not linked. The stock price falling to $20 doesn't mean the dividend goes away.

When the stock price was $40, your $33 of dividend income purchased an extra 0.83 shares. With the price now at $20, your dividend re-investment buys twice as many shares. An extra 1.65 shares after year #1.

In the 2nd year, your dividend income would be $37.31. If the stock stays at $20, that's good for another 1.86 shares. The lower the price, the more shares you can buy. Simple, right? So if the price stays at $20 - you're going to get rich real quick.

When Coca-Cola's stock price stayed at $40, you were able to accumulate 73.6 shares over 20 years. With the stock price at $20 for the entire period, you would be able to build up an astounding 244 shares! The following chart illustrates your share count growth over time.

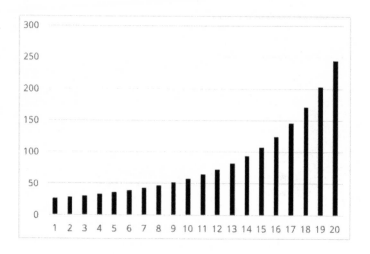

That nets you $4,381 in total dividend income. In Year #20 alone, you received $812 – an 81% return on your initial investment in a single year!

That's not even the best part.

The value of your shares at the end of year #20 is higher at $20 per share than it would be if the stock had remained at $40. Your Coca-Cola stock would be worth $4,069 – quadruple your initial investment!

Do you see the absurdity of this? The dividend strategy is so robust that you quadruple your money even though stock prices fell by 50%.

Is This Realistic?

If you're reading about this strategy for the first time, you might think it sounds too good to be true. It's not. In fact, it gets better.

Not only do dividend stocks provide the opportunity, but you can do it with a high degree of success.

If you watch the financial media much, you'll hear them brag about a "triple bagger" they called. They'll tout the next [insert social media or fancy tech stock here] that's going to triple in value.

Here's the problem. Picking the next Facebook, Microsoft, or Google isn't likely. Even if you do eventually hit a home run on an investment, you likely had plenty of strike outs trying to find it.

Picking winning tech/social media/pharma stocks is like gambling at the casino. You might hit it big once or twice, but the longer you play, the more certain you will lose.

Dividend growth investing is the opposite. The more you "play," the better your odds. You don't even have to pick winners before they become winners. Identify companies that are already winning. Buy them for their growing dividend income stream. You won't triple your money overnight with these companies, but you will eventually.

You were able to triple your $1,000 investment in Coca-Cola without much effort. All we did was predict that Coca-Cola is going to continue growing their dividend over the next 20 years. That seems likely considering they've raised the dividend for 52 consecutive years.

Why would the next 20 be any different?

We didn't assume any crazy growth rates, either. Coca-Cola has grown their dividend by more than 6% in the past. No one applauded Coca-Cola for their dividend in any of those years. Their CEO was never on CNBC promoting the next big product launch. It was boring and predictable.

I don't know about you, but I prefer my investments to be boring and predictable. Dividend growth investing takes the pressure off you to pick winning stocks. Let the power of growing dividends do all the work for you.

It is possible for you to build wealth without jumping in and out of stocks or "timing the market." A growing stream of dividend income is the investment answer you have been seeking.

Back to Jim and Sally

Let's say Jim and Sally pick up a copy of this book and decide that dividend growth investing is for them. If their advisor is not an expert in dividend growth investing, they can transfer the money to someone who is.

Jim and Sally buy shares in 30 dividend growth stocks with an average dividend yield of 3%. Their portfolio consists of companies that they know and love.

In the first year, Jim and Sally collect $15,000 in dividend income. The cash is automatically paid into their bank accounts on a monthly basis - just like a paycheck.

In year #2, Jim and Sally receive a 6% pay increase. The $15,000 worth of dividends last year increases to $15,900 next year. Then it grows again in the 3rd year.

The following chart shows how the dividends growing at 6% grow faster than their spending.

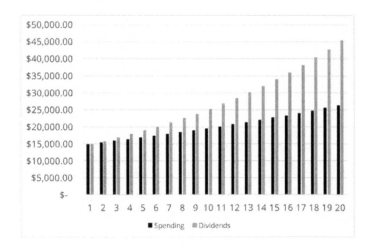

After 20 years, Jim and Sally will be spending $26,300 per year. Their dividend income would be $45,300 per year. And the best part? They didn't have to sell a single share of stock to earn that rising income!

What About Market Value?

As long as Jim and Sally spend only the dividend income, they don't have to worry about market prices moving up or down. Mr. Market no longer has any control over their lives.

He still offers them a new price on their dividend stocks every single day, but they never take him up on it. They are content to hold onto their shares of high-quality dividend stocks. Why would they sell? As long as they keep collecting the cash dividends, owning these companies is a no-brainer.

Dividend growth investing enabled Jim and Sally to grow their income and sleep well at night. They have taken care of their expenses regardless of what Mr. Market's mood is on that particular day. Not only that, but Jim and Sally have never touched the principal. They will have a large inheritance that they will be able to leave to their children.

There will be doubters. A lot of people out there that will tell you that owning a portfolio of individual stocks is pointless. "You should buy an index fund and forget about it," they'll say.

We'll talk about that in the next chapter.

7

CAN DIVIDENDS BEAT
THE INDEX?

"I believe non-dividend stocks aren't much more than baseball cards. They are worth what you can convince someone to pay for it." –Mark Cuban

Before we entertain the idea of whether or not a portfolio of dividend growth stocks will "beat the index" or not, let's take a step back. Ask yourself this: What is the ultimate goal of your investment portfolio?

If the S&P 500 index returns 15% next year and you only get 13%, will you feel like the year was a failure?

If you collected $50,000 in dividend income last year, would you care what the S&P 500 did?

Is beating the S&P 500 really your goal? If so, then dividend investing might not be for you. Maybe you should just put your money in an S&P 500 index and forget about it. If your goal is to meet your real-life spending needs, then stay tuned.

If you're still with me, then you've decided you don't care too much about the S&P 500. Your goal is really to replace your paycheck one day with a stream of growing dividend income. Whether you earn a 7% return or a 12% return is irrelevant as long as you can pay the bills each month and sleep well at night.

Ok, I'm skirting around the original question here. Let's get to it: Can you beat the S&P 500 investing in dividend growth stocks?

The answer is a resounding yes! It is possible to outperform the S&P 500 index with a portfolio of high-quality dividend growth stocks. I've seen it done by individual investors and corporations, alike.

However, what about the research showing that mutual funds underperform index funds over the long-term? It is true. The average mutual fund will underperform a simple S&P 500 index fund over a long period of time. If are deciding between a mutual fund and an index fund, you should take the index fund 99 times out of 100.

If a highly trained mutual fund manager can't beat the index, how on Earth is it possible to do better than them? It's a lot more likely than you think.

By investing in individual stocks, you have several significant advantages over Wall Street's mutual fund managers.

1. No mutual fund fees

When you or your investment advisor puts your money in mutual funds, there is an additional cost of around 0.61% per year[18], on average. You don't notice this fee because it comes out of the funds' earnings – but it is there.

---

[18] Oey, Patricia. "Average Fund Costs Continue to Decline in 2015." Morningstar, April 2016.

Mutual funds are doubly expensive if they come with sales loads. This can cost between 5% and 8% of your investment right up front. So an initial investment of $100,000 will only end up worth about $95,000 after your investment advisor skims $5,000 off the top.

If you add an investment advisor fee on top of fund costs, you're looking at recurring fees of around 1.61% per year. That is on top of one-time sales loads that can be as high as 5.4% for stock funds and 3.8% for bond funds[19].

And that doesn't even include commissions, account fees, or any other of the costs associated with mutual fund investing.

By purchasing individual stocks yourself or through your advisor, you have a head start on the average person that invests in mutual funds.

---

[19] "Mutual Fund Expenses and Fees." 2016 Investment Company Fact Book.

2. Direct ownership

When you own individual companies, you get to own the stocks directly in your investment account. When you own a mutual fund or index fund, on the other hand, you have no idea what's in your portfolio. And you certainly don't have control over what is bought or sold.

Owning individual stocks also allows you to receive your dividend income directly from the company. When you own an index fund or mutual fund, you don't own the underlying companies. You just own the vehicle that owns them. That means the fund has control over the dividends and when to distribute them.

Individual stocks also mean you will get paid more frequently. If you own a portfolio of 30-50 individual stocks, you will get paid somewhere between 120 and 200 dividends over the course of a year. Contrast that with most mutual funds, who only distribute dividends out once every three months.

More frequent payments means two things:

First, it is easier to pay your bills

If you're retired and living on your dividend income, would you prefer to get four paychecks per year or 200? The more checks, the better.

Secondly, your money compounds faster

Receiving more frequent income allows you to reinvest the dividends faster. This is called "compounding." The faster your money compounds, the more it grows over time.

The difference between monthly and quarterly compounding can be a big deal over time. A $500,000 investment compounded monthly would grow $16,000 larger over a 20 year period.

3. Higher income

The average large-cap mutual fund offers a dividend yield somewhere in the neighborhood of 2% before fees are taken out. After the average mutual fund fee, most investors end up with a dividend yield around 1.4%.

In some small-cap mutual funds, the end investor may not end up with a dividend at all!

Unfortunately, buying index funds doesn't offer much help. At the time of writing, the SPDR S&P 500 index fund (SPY) offers a dividend yield of just 2.01%[20].

4. Own higher quality stocks

The primary argument for investing in index funds is diversification. The idea is to spread your money across as many different companies as possible. That way, if one goes under - you won't notice that much. This makes sense from a mathematical perspective, but not from a business perspective.

---

[20] Source: Morningstar, December 2016.

Think about the companies in your hometown. Do you believe those businesses all make the same amount of money? Of course not. Some companies make money hand over fist, while others barely scrape by. Some have a loyal customer base while others struggle to get people in the door.

If given a choice between owning a little bit of all the businesses (both good and bad) or holding only the best, which would you choose? Of course, you would prefer to own more of the best businesses and less of the bad ones.

If you would prefer to own only the best businesses in your hometown, why would you not prefer the same in your investment account?

Higher quality companies that make more money will result in better investment returns over time. Research backs this up. High-quality dividend-paying companies tend to fall less in bad markets. During the Great Recession of 2008-09, the S&P 500 dropped by 37% while the US Dividend Achievers only declined in value by 26.5%[21].

By investing in dividend stocks, you will be selecting from the highest quality stocks available. As we mentioned earlier, less than 10% of the available US stocks have raised their dividends for 3+ years. And less than 2% have increased them for 10+ years. If you focus on dividend growth, you are automatically selecting from the top 0.8% of all stocks out there.

5. Dividend stocks outperform non-dividend-paying stocks

Since 1972, companies that paid a dividend have dramatically outperformed those who have not.

---

[21] US Dividend Achievers represented by the Vanguard Dividend Appreciation Index Fund ETF (VIG), Source: Morningstar.

A $100 investment in non-dividend payers would have lost money - down to $99. Those who had paid a dividend but cut or eliminated it fared better, but not much - growing $100 to $264. The dividend payers who paid a dividend but did not increase it grew $100 to $2,199. The difference between paying a dividend and not paying a dividend was 10x!

The next chart shows the difference between dividend stocks and dividend cutters or non-payers over time:

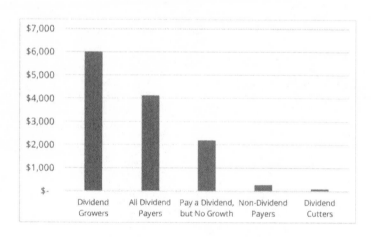

However, it gets even better. Those companies that not only paid a dividend but increased it in that year grew a $100 investment to $5,997[22]!

Which would you rather invest in? Every single stock in the entire market? Or a select few that consistently grow their dividends year-after-year?

6. Think longer term

I feel sorry for mutual fund managers. Not because they aren't paid enough, but their jobs are hard.

The culture on Wall Street is to obsess over performance numbers. If a mutual fund underperforms its benchmark in any given year (even three months), investors move their money to a different fund. The manager could even be fired if that fund underperforms the benchmark for a few years in a row.

---

[22] "S&P 500 Index: Dividend Growers Have Outperformed Over Time"
Hypothetical Performance of $100 invested in each of the five strategies (1972-2013). Source: Ned Davis Research, 12/31/13

This focus on short-term results forces mutual fund managers to make short-term decisions. The manager might make changes that hurt results over the next 20 years to make investors stick around.

If you own a portfolio of individual stocks, you are free from the pressures of Wall Street. You don't need to answer to anyone about your performance over a three month period. That allows you to make decisions focused on the next ten years rather than one.

A long-term focus lets you ignore a company's short-term results. If a business misses Wall Street's expectations for its earnings per share by even one penny, it could have its stock price crushed by 5% or more in a day. An "earnings beat" could drive the stock the other way in a matter of seconds.

As a dividend investor, you aren't a slave to earnings reports or short-term fluctuations. Over time, these things will even out.

Focusing on the dividend allows you to think about what drives stock prices over the long-term: dividend growth. A 10% increase in the dividend indicates that management is confident that it can continue to pay that dividend indefinitely. If management were not confident in the future, they would not increase the dividend. That makes dividends a true indicator of a company's long-term outlook.

7. Minimal trading costs

Mutual funds and short-term investors ("traders") are always buying and selling stocks. All this activity leads to high trading costs and lower returns. A long-term focus allows you to reduce trading costs to virtually nothing.

Trading costs come in two forms: (1) commission charges from the brokerage firm and (2) bid-ask spread costs.

The commission charge is typically somewhere between $5-10 per trade. That doesn't sound like much, but it adds up over time. A mutual fund might make tens or hundreds of trades each day. This adds up to thousands of dollars in costs that are paid by who, exactly? You, of course!

Another cost of trading is called the "bid-ask spread." When you make a transaction on the stock market, there is always a small difference between what price the buyer is willing to pay and what the seller is willing to sell. This spread means that both the buyer and seller take a cut off of each trade. This cut is often just a few pennies. Over time, however, these pennies add up to big bucks.

In a study of 1,758 mutual funds, researchers concluded that trading costs add up to an average of 1.44% per year[23] for the average mutual fund investor. That is even more than what they pay in expense ratios and other fees!

If you own individual dividend stocks, you'll pay a $5 or $10 commission when you or your advisor purchases the stock, but you may not pay another cent for another 5, 10, and even 20 years! Over the same period, a mutual fund manager would rack up hundreds of thousands of dollars in commission costs.

---

[23] Edelen, Evans & Kadlec, "Shedding Light on 'Invisible' Costs: Trading Costs and Mutual Fund Performance." Financial Analysts Journal, January/February 2013, Volume 69 Issue 1.

While the fund managers frantically click on their trading screens, you'll be cashing those dividend checks.

8. Lower taxes

Mutual funds have no real incentive to watch out for your tax bill. Their performance numbers don't consider the tax implications of their regular trading and short-term gains. They only care about what return they get before taxes. That is the number that gets reported in all the investor brochures.

As an investor, you shouldn't care about the headline number. The only thing that counts for you is what your net return is after you pay all taxes and costs. On a 10% gain, you might only see 8% of that after taxes.

If you have a portfolio of individual stocks, you can be more strategic about when to buy and sell for tax purposes. That could save you between 10 and 15% on your taxes each year. You can also use what's called "tax loss harvesting" to offset gains with losses - meaning you'll be making money but not paying a dime in tax!

9. Ignore Mr. Market

Let's consider a mutual fund manager that does a detailed analysis and decides that a stock is worth $100 per share. If the stock is trading at $50, the mutual fund manager would consider it a "buy" and add it to the fund.

The problem is that Mr. Market doesn't always agree. If the company misses their next earnings numbers, Mr. Market might only offer $40 per share. If Mr. Market gets extremely pessimistic, he might push the stock price to $20 or lower.

It's hard to stare down Mr. Market as he continues to rate your shares lower and lower in value. Without a dividend, the investment does not become profitable unless someone else is willing to pay more than $500 in the future. Will that happen? Maybe. However, it also may not.

As a dividend investor, you can insulate yourself from Mr. Market's mood swings. If you buy shares in Coca-Cola at $40 per share, and Mr. Market re-prices those shares to $35, you don't mind. You're still receiving $1.32 per share in dividend income each year.

And that income continues to grow even if the stock price falls! Even if Mr. Market never prices Coca-Cola's stock above $35, you continue collecting your dividend checks every year.

10. Get 100% of your dividend income

When you invest in individual stocks, you are the direct shareholder in the company. That means you get all dividend income directly to your account. When Coca-Cola pays its $0.33 quarterly dividend, you receive that on the pay date and not a day later.

With a fund, those dividends first pass through a third-party investment company. So Coca-Cola's dividend checks go to the mutual fund first. Then they get distributed to the shareholders at the fund's discretion. Rather than receiving checks directly from the companies, you have to wait until the fund pays once every three months or so.

Even If You Do Not Beat the Index

Let's assume just for a moment that you can look into the future and see that your portfolio of dividend stocks will underperform the S&P 500 index.

Even if that's the case, you may still earn a higher overall return than you would following the typical fund strategy.

How is that possible? I'll show you.

Let's say you are 40 years old starting with a $250,000 portfolio. A traditional index fund strategy would have you put your age into a bond index fund and the rest into a stock index fund.

According to this rule of thumb, a 40-year-old would put 40% of their investment portfolio in bonds. The other 60% would go into stocks. Each year, the investor would reduce their stock allocation by 1% and move that into bonds - getting more conservative over time.

Let's assume that the S&P 500 index fund returns 8%, and the bond fund returns 3%, both in line with Vanguard's estimates for the next ten years. A portfolio starting with 60% stocks and 40% bonds would grow by 5.70% per year.

As a dividend investor, your 40-year-old self isn't interested in bonds at this point. You want to grow your future dividend income so that it will eventually cover your expenses. Bonds are going to slow you down. So you go with 100% dividend stocks.

Let's say your portfolio underperforms the S&P 500 by 1%, returning just 7% per year instead of 8%. That would be disappointing, but you would still achieve a higher realized return than the index fund investor.

Why? Because the index fund investor-owned bonds that only produced around 3% per year. So even though the return for their stocks were 8%, the return of their overall portfolio was just 5.75%. That's still 1.25% lower than yours!

One of the key advantages you have over a traditional indexing strategy is that a dividend investor has little need for bonds. We'll talk more about that in the next chapter.

Over an extended period (5+ years), it is possible to outperform the S&P 500 index. Will you or I beat the market over the next year or two? I don't know. What I do know is that you will have collected a ton of cash over that period, and that dividend income will continue to grow.

8

ARE DIVIDENDS RIGHT FOR ME?

"Our goals can only be reached through a vehicle of a plan in which we must fervently believe, and upon which we must vigorously act. There is no other route to success." —Pablo Picasso

In all of my 10+ years of investment experience, I have yet to find a strategy that works nearly as well as buying and holding a portfolio of high-quality dividend growth stocks. It offers investors several key advantages that we have touched on in this book.

Outperform the S&P 500 index

Since 1972, companies that have grown their dividends outperform the average stock by more than 3x.

Past performance is not an indicator of future returns, but it does indicate that dividend-paying companies have historically done quite well over extremely long periods (30+ years).

Less price volatility

In 2008, the S&P 500 fell by 39%. The Dividend Achievers (10+ years of dividend growth) decreased by only 25%. To achieve the same risk profile with index funds, you would have to own 30% bonds, which reduces future returns.

Higher realized future returns

Since a dividend investor doesn't need to own as many bonds, they can outperform the average investor, even if they don't do a good job of picking stocks! A 100% dividend stock portfolio that underperforms the S&P 500 index by 1% per year is still likely to beat an 80/20 stock/bond portfolio of index funds!

Higher current income

The S&P 500 index produces a dividend yield of approximately 1.9% at the time of this writing. A high-quality dividend portfolio would generate close to 3% or more. That's more income to live on now or re-invest into ever more streams of growing dividends.

Little chance of losing money over the long-term

If a dividend growth portfolio starts with a dividend yield of 3% and grows by 6% per year, it has little chance of losing money over a 20 year period.

Income that grows faster than inflation

Dividend growth stocks continue to increase their dividends year-after-year, usually faster than inflation. Bonds and annuities, on the other hand, have flat income.

Emotional anchor

Focusing on dividends rather than market prices helps you stick with your strategy when stock prices are down, rather than panicking and selling at the bottom like so many of your friends will do.

Is building a dividend growth portfolio worth it? You bet it is! Focusing on the constant fluctuation of stock prices and your account value is not a good way to invest.

A dividend investor can ignore falling stock prices (even cheer for them!) and look towards building a stream of consistent, reliable, and growing income for many years to come. These dividend payments can be reinvested to produce great masses of wealth or used to fund your living expenses once you stop earning a paycheck.

PART THREE
APPLYING THE
DIVIDEND STRATEGY

In the final Part of the book, we'll get into the practical application. If you want to add dividends to your portfolio, how exactly do you go about doing it?

In Chapter 9, we'll look at some examples of companies with long dividend histories. Please note this is not a recommended portfolio, but is merely an example of the kinds of companies you might consider.

Chapter 10, we'll do a brief introduction to dividend ETFs and how dividend stocks or funds might fit in your 401(k) or other employer-sponsored retirement account.

Chapter 11 will give you some thoughts on hiring a financial advisor. I'll give you some points to consider when determining whether you need some help or not.

If you're planning to hire an advisor, Chapter 12 will help you find someone that is qualified, competent, ethical, and — most importantly — legally required to give you the best advice they know how. I would encourage anyone who has or is planning to hire an advisor to send this list of questions to candidates.

And, finally, I'll provide a list of additional resources that you might find helpful.

After that, the book is over. I'll give you my contact information and then tell you a little bit about me — if you care! I'll re-iterate that I would love to hear from you. So please email me your thoughts on the book.

9

THE DIVIDEND KINGS

"The thing is, if you're just oogling fat current dividend yields you are missing the more profitable boat. When it comes to dividend investing, the far smarter play is to zero in on companies that consistently increase their dividend payouts." –Wealthifi

Johnny's Lemonade Stand was a hypothetical example of a company that paid a dividend each year to its shareholders. There are hundreds of real businesses that do the same thing. More than 400 companies in the S&P 500 currently pay a dividend.

However, that doesn't necessarily mean that all 400+ would be worth your investment dollars.

Keep in mind that dividend payments are optional. The company's management team decides how much (if any) dividend they will pay. The dividend may be reduced or stopped altogether if the business runs into hard times.

Company management does not want to cut the dividend because it often leads to disaster for their stock price, but there are certain cases were they have no choice.

Take Kinder Morgan (KMI), for example. At the beginning of 2015, you could buy a share of KMI for around $42. In 2015, Kinder paid out $3.32 in dividends. If you had bought $100 worth of KMI's stock, you would have expected to receive $8 in dividends. That's an 8% return from the dividend alone!

Who wouldn't want to invest in them?

Unfortunately, commodity prices (oil and natural gas) plummeted in 2015. Kinder Morgan's business prospects declined with them. Not only that, but Kinder Morgan had loaded up their company with lots of debt to pay for future growth projects. It was not a good combination. Within just 12 months, Kinder Morgan's business eroded so fast that they were forced to cut their dividend by 75%.

The 8% dividend yield at the beginning of 2015 ended up at around 2% by year-end. Not only that, but the stock price fell by more than 65%. By the end of 2015, your $100 investment in KMI would have been worth just $35.

That's why just finding companies that pay dividends is not enough. The best strategy is to look for companies that not only pay a dividend but those that have a high probability of continuing to pay one in the future and grow it each and every year. Those are the companies that will build long-term wealth for you and me!

We don't want to own a bunch of companies that pay high dividends but have poor prospects for future dividend growth. These stocks have high dividend yields (even 10%+) but aren't worth buying.

Why not? Chances are pretty strong that those dividends will be cut in the future. At the very least, they won't increase year-after-year.

We want to buy the kinds of companies that have incredible businesses that we can rely on to pay us a generous dividend today and keep growing that dividend for the next 10, 20, 30 years. Few companies are good enough to sustain this kind of growth. Most will be killed by global competitors, better products, or poor management.

That's why dividend growth is such a reliable measure of quality. If a company can afford to grow its dividend for 10, 25, even 50 years in a row, they have to be doing something right. They have a product or products that are in high demand and will likely continue to be in demand in the future - no matter what happens to the economy, technology, or investor sentiment.

The ability to pay and grow a dividend automatically eliminates most non-quality companies.

Consider that there are currently 12,419 stocks available for purchase on US stock exchanges. We can whittle those down pretty quickly using dividends as a screening tool.

- Out of the 12,419 available stocks, only 2,092 of those 12,419 currently pay a dividend (16.8%).[24]
- Just 1,172 were able to grow their dividend over the last three years (9.4%).[25]
- A minuscule 183 were able to grow their dividends over the last ten years. That's less than 1.5% of the available 12,419 stocks.[26]
- And just 18 companies have been able to grow their dividends for 50 consecutive years. That's less than 0.15% of stocks.[27]

To get an idea of what kind of companies were are looking at, let's meet the list of 18 "Dividend Kings."

---

[24] Source: Bloomberg Terminal.

[25] Source: Bloomberg Terminal.

[26] Source: Bloomberg Terminal.

[27] Source: Bloomberg Terminal.

The Dividend Kings

There are currently 18 companies that have paid and raised their dividend each and every year for 25+ years. These are the types of stocks that we can use to build incredible wealth over time.

From 1991 through 2015, the S&P 500 index returned 9.8% per year.[28] That would grow a $1 investment to $10.45.

An equal investment in each of the 18 Dividend Kings would have generated a return of 14.0% per year. That would grow a $1 investment to $26.67.

Here is the list of companies. You'll probably recognize a few.

American States Water (AWR) is a water and electricity utility in California.

---

[28] "Dividend Stocks with 50+ Years of Rising Dividends." Sure Dividend, October 2016.

Cincinnati Financial (CINF) provides insurance to companies and individuals.

Colgate-Palmolive (CL) makes Colgate toothpaste, Speed Stick deodorant, Palmolive dish soap, and even cat food.

Dover Corporation (DOV) is a conglomerate industrial manufacturer.

Emerson Electric (EMR) makes process automation technologies, climate technologies, and commercial/residential tools.

Farmers and Merchants Bancorp (FMCB) is a community bank chain located exclusively in California.

Genuine Parts (GPC) makes automotive parts and owns retail auto repair shops. You might recognize them as NAPA Auto Care.

Hormel Foods (HRL) owns brands Wholly Guacamole, Muscle Milk, Skippy peanut butter, Hormel, and everyone's favorite unrecognizable meat product (Spam).

Johnson & Johnson (JNJ) owns your medicine cabinet. Seriously. They include Motrin, Tylenol, Benadryl, Zyrtec, Band-Aid, Listerine, Aveeno, Neutrogena, and Johnson's. They also make medical devices and have a pharmaceutical division.

Coca-Cola (KO) makes sugar water and a whole lot more. You might recognize their Dasani and Vitamin Water brands in addition to Minute Maid, Fuze, Gold Peak, Schweppes, Simply Orange, Honest T, Powerade, and more.

Lancaster Colony (LNC) sells regional specialty food products such as bread.

Lowe's (LOW) is a US home improvement retail store.

3M (MMM) makes everything from paint supplies to Post-It Notes.

Nordson (NDSN) is another industrial manufacturer.

Northwest Natural Gas (NWN) is a natural gas utility in Oregon and Washington.

Parker-Hannifan (PH) is a diversified industrial goods manufacturer.

Procter & Gamble (PG) owns everything else in your house that you don't buy from Johnson & Johnson. Their brands include Crest, Tide, Pampers, Head & Shoulders, Gillette, and many others.

Vectren (VVC) is a gas and electric utility in Indiana and Ohio. I pay my utility bill to them. If you own their stock, you're   welcome.

I'm not suggesting that all or even most of these companies are a good investment today. Not all 18 of these companies will pay a dividend for the next 50 years. But you can bet that most of them will continue for many years to come.

When you are looking for a good investment for the future, companies that have historically grown their dividends for several years in a row are typically better investments than those that have not.

10

HOW TO START YOUR OWN DIVIDEND PORTFOLIO

"The investor's chief problem and even his worst enemy is likely to be himself." -Benjamin Graham

So far, the book has been more about why the dividend strategy is so powerful. But how do you go about implementing it?

You have a few options.

Dividend Funds

If you're just starting out, managing a portfolio of individual dividend stocks probably doesn't make sense. The commission charges to buy a stock currently run from $5 to $10.

To own a diversified portfolio of 10-30 stocks, you're going to pay at least $50 to $150 just to get started. If your account is only $1,000 – those charges are going to subtract 5% to 15% from your initial investment. It will take you years to overcome those costs.

If you have $10,000 or less to invest, you should start by purchasing some dividend-focused mutual funds or exchange-traded funds (ETFs).

My personal favorite is the Vanguard High Dividend Yield ETF (VYM). You'll own approximately 300 stocks with a nice combination of high yield, dividend growth, and strong performance.

While you're buying dividend funds and adding to your account each month, I would suggest reading more books about stock selection. Start with Benjamin Graham's "Security Analysis". It may be a bit technical at first, but it will provide a solid foundation for you.

A Word on 401(k) Assets

One reader asked me about implementing a dividend strategy in her employer's 401(k).

If you have money in a 401(k), 403(b), or other retirement account sponsored by your employer – you probably won't have access to a dividend fund or individual stocks. You are limited to the menu of mutual funds offered by the plan.

In this situation, your best bet is to find a low-cost fund that tracks the US stock market. This is most likely going to be an S&P 500 Index fund. If you're having trouble with your options, ask around for a fee-only financial advisor. They may be willing to help you identify a good option for you.

If you have an old 401(k) at a previous employer, you can do an "IRA Rollover" which simply means moving money out of the old account and putting it into an IRA in your name. This will open up your investment options to allow you to invest in anything you want.

Individual Stocks

As your portfolio grows larger (and so does your knowledge), you may want to start buying individual dividend stocks.

This is by no means an exhaustive "how to". This book is not focused on stock selection. My goal with this book was to give you a short, easy-to-read introduction to dividends. There are other books[29] out there that would be helpful for you with respect to stock analysis. In this chapter, I'll give you a few thoughts that I hope will help get you started.

---

[29] "Security Analysis" by Benjamin Graham, "The Single Best Investment" by Lowell Miller, "The Snowball Effect" by Timothy J McIntosh, "Berkshire Hathaway Letters to Shareholders" by Warren Buffett and Max Olson, "The Ultimate Dividend Playbook: Income, Insight and Independence for Today's Investor" by Morningstar and Josh Peters.

1. Focus on Dividend Growth more than Dividend Yield.

Too many investors fall in love with ultra-high yielding stocks. A high dividend yield usually indicates a low-quality, high-risk company. Most stocks with yields of 6% and higher are being priced for a dividend cut. At minimum, they are being priced for low future dividend growth.

A stock with a 2% dividend yield and 10% dividend growth will ultimately produce more dividend income than a stock with a 6% dividend yield and 0% dividend growth. And quite a bit more than a 20% yielding stock that will (eventually) have to cut their dividend.

Don't fall in love with yield. You want sustainable, low-risk, predictable dividend growth for many years to come. Don't get too greedy for dividends now.

2. Pay Attention to Payout Ratios.

Dividends ultimately are paid out of cash flows. A company that pays out more in dividends than it brings in will eventually be forced to reduce the dividend.

Before you buy a stock, be sure to check the payout ratio. That is simply the amount paid in dividends divided by the earnings generated over the past year.

A company with a payout ratio of 80% is paying out $8 in dividends for every $10 in earnings. A company with a 20% payout ratio is paying out $2 for every $10 in earnings.

Which company will have more room for future dividend growth? It's the 20% payout ratio. Not only do they have more room to pay dividends, they also have more money left to reinvest in the business.

A company with a payout ratio of 100% or more should be avoided. Unless earnings increase, the dividend will eventually be cut.

3. Watch Out for Financial Shenanigans.

There are lots of companies out there that recognize how attractive the dividend is for investors. To support their stock price, they "pump" the dividend artificially.

This can be done a number of ways. First, the company can issue lots of debt to maintain their unsustainable dividend. Second, the company can raise money by selling their own stock to other investors. This dilutes current shareholders and offsets – even completely eliminates – the value of the dividend.

To find out if a company is issuing equity or debt, you can look at their financial statements. Those are available on many different websites, but I would suggest Morningstar for quality data over the past 5 years.

4. Pay Attention to Stock Prices.

Investing is like physics. An object in motion tends to stay in motion. Research has proven that near-term price momentum over the past 3 to 18 months tends to continue.

In other words, a stock that has been falling in value for the past year will likely continue to fall. This doesn't always hold, but plenty of academic papers confirm this phenomenon.

The lesson for you is clear: Don't try to "catch a falling knife". A "falling knife" is a stock that has been declining in price dramatically.

Rather than buying them on the way down, it can be a good practice to put them on a "watch list" until the price starts to show some stability or upward movement. These companies can often present good long-term opportunities, but near-term trends can be hard to break.

Using some simple moving averages can help you with this. For example, let's say you identify a stock you really like – but the price is heading straight down. Put it on a list. When the stock price rises above, say, the 50 or 200-day moving average – consider buying it.

SIDE NOTE: A "moving average" is simply the average of a stock's price over the past n number of days. For example, if Apple's stock trades at $180 yesterday and $190 today, its 2-day moving average would be $185. Moving averages help smooth out the noise in stock prices and are useful for identifying changes in price trends.

Following this moving average strategy means you won't buy a stock at the absolute bottom, but that's not the goal. Your goal should be to get it at a good – not perfect – price. Whatever possible price gains you miss out on will be more than made up for by the number of doozies you avoid.

11

SHOULD I HIRE A FINANCIAL ADVISOR?

Another option you have to implement a dividend strategy is to hire an advisor to help you.

"Unfortunately, the vast majority of those who bill themselves as financial advisors neither charge a fair price nor give good advice. More than any other market I know, the market for financial advice is 'let the buyer beware.'" —Jim Dahle, M.D.

Several readers have asked me about hiring a financial advisor to help them implement a dividend strategy. If you don't have the time, interest, or skills to buy dividend stocks on your own — a financial advisor may be able to help build a solid portfolio for you and (most importantly) keep you on track.

This is a controversial topic. Some people have had bad experiences with advisors in the past and want nothing to do with them again. Others have had great experiences and actively promote their advisor to friends and family.

But this isn't a question for anyone else. It's a question for you. And it's an important one. In some cases, it can be the difference between financial success and failure. Don't take it lightly.

So — do you need to hire a financial advisor?

If you had asked me this question a few years ago, my answer to that would almost certainly be "No". Investors could surely educate themselves enough to manage their own financial affairs, right?

In a perfect world, yes. We would all create detailed budgets every month and stick with them.

We would all know exactly how much we need to save for retirement. We would then save the exact amount we needed each month to get there. We would all minimize our taxes and prepare our own estate plans. We would also have perfect knowledge about stocks, bonds, and real estate. We would know what percentage of each we should buy of each.

We would all buy stocks in 2008 after they've dropped by more than 50%. No one would panic at the bottom and sell everything. We would all stop reading the financial news and watching CNBC for the latest market opinion.

If everyone did the above, then there is no need for advisors. Paying someone a financial planning fee or investment management fee would be a complete waste of money.

However, most people simply don't do those things. Most of us wallow in debt, make unnecessary purchases, and find every excuse possible to avoid making a budget.

Once we start investing, we do dumb things. We buy penny stocks, read newsletters promising to "double your money in 3 months." We fill our portfolios with high yielding Master Limited Partnership (MLP) stocks in 2015, then get killed when they all cut their dividends and prices drop by 50%.

We have a job at a publicly traded company and put half of our 401(k) assets in that company's stock. Then when the company falls on hard times, our jobs get cut at the same time our 401(k) values get crushed.

We fall for the latest investment fads like buying Technology stocks in 2000, mortgage-backed securities in 2008, Energy stocks in 2015, and FAANG stocks in 2018. All end badly.

We chase the best performing mutual funds, only to watch them be the worst performing funds the next few years. We prognosticate when we should get out of the market. We constantly worry about the "next bubble" in stocks.

Rinse. Repeat.

We don't live in a perfect world. And none of us – myself included – are anywhere near an optimal financial situation.

After speaking with individual investors and working with hundreds of clients, I'm convinced that it takes a special kind of person to manage their own investment portfolio.

I'm not saying you aren't smart enough to manage their own investments. In fact, I would argue that you are plenty smart enough. If you're reading this book — or any investing book — you're probably plenty smart. The problem is less about intelligence and more about your emotions.

People think they act rationally with their money and investments, but they don't. You don't. And I don't, either.

The Real Value of an Advisor

When you hire an advisor, you're not necessarily hiring someone for their ability to pick stocks or provide the perfect mix of stocks and bonds for your situation. Someone well-educated and well-read in finance can do that.

You're not even really hiring them to build a financial plan for you and tell you what to do to get there. Although, that is part of it.

What you're *really* hiring them to do is to be a coach to be there when things get difficult. When your stocks drop in value by 20%, a good advisor will help keep avoid making a bad decision.

A third-party advisor doesn't have the same emotional attachment to your money that you do. He or she can help you develop an investment plan, yes, but their most important job is **to help you stick with it over time without doing something stupid.**

When you're young and just starting out, these bad decisions aren't as costly. A $10,000 portfolio that drops in half only loses $5,000.

As your accounts get bigger, so do the stakes. A retired person's $500,000 portfolio has a lot more money at risk than their grandson's $10,000 Roth IRA. Not only that, but one bad mistake can be the difference between a long, happy retirement and relying exclusively on Social Security to pay the bills.

So, should you hire an advisor? At the end of the day, it comes down to answering this question: **Will your advisor add enough to your financial future to offset the cost of their services?**

If not, then you should manage your own money. Or possibly consider paying an hourly fee to a financial planner when you need a little tax or planning help.

If an advisor adds more value than they cost, then you should hire one. More tips on that in a minute.

First, here's a checklist of things to think about before hiring an advisor to help you.

Does My Investment Performance Beat the Advisor?

If you are able to earn better returns than the advisor after paying their fees, then you should consider managing your own portfolio. If not, then hiring an advisor is a no-brainer.

To find out, you should compare how you have done vs. what the advisor you are considering hiring has done.

If you made 15% last year and would have made 16% with the advisor, you would be just as well off paying them a 1% fee. The 16% minus 1% fee would be 15% - the same return that you got.

If you made 15% last year and the advisor made 17% with a 1% fee, then the cost of the advisor is positive – not negative.

Can the advisor help me save on taxes, interest, or other expenses?

Most accountants are too busy filing taxes to really do much tax planning for people. A competent financial advisor can help fill the gaps.

For example, what is the most tax-efficient way for you to withdraw money in retirement? Should you take from the Roth IRA first or the Traditional IRA? And where do the taxable accounts come in?

Can the advisor help me sleep better at night?

If you are constantly worrying about your portfolio, a good advisor can help you design a portfolio that fits your risk tolerance. They can also help keep you calm during inevitable market events.

Can the advisor save me time?

How long does it take you to manage your portfolio each year? How much time do you spend analyzing retirement calculators? What about reading articles about the markets?

If you didn't have to do as many of these things, how much time would that save you? Is that time savings worth what the advisor is charging?

Does the advisor share my investment philosophy?

After reading this book, you may be interested in hiring an advisor to help you select individual dividend stocks or funds. If the advisor has no experience or expertise with dividend stocks, you may prefer to manage your own investments.

Add It All Up

Once you add it all up, you may find that an advisor is not worth the price you're going to pay. You may find that you're just as capable of doing it on your own. Or you may find that you'd benefit from working with someone.

It's your choice. Don't let anyone pressure you into making a decision. It's not a small one. The person you hire will help direct you to a successful financial outcome. You need to make sure they are a good fit for you. And you need to absolutely be sure they are worth the fees you are going to pay them for their expertise.

If you do decide to hire an advisor, how do you know whether you're getting a good one or not? I'm glad you asked. More on that in the next chapter.

12

QUESTIONS TO ASK A FINANCIAL ADVISOR

"Fiduciaries disclose all fees including the fees associated with investment recommendations. They should have few or no conflicts. For any unavoidable conflicts, they disclose it in full and explain what it means." —Jane Bryant Quinn

Before you hire a financial advisor, you need to be sure you know some detailed information on their investment strategy, financial planning offerings, fees, and past investment performance.

Below are 19 questions you should ask any advisor you're considering hiring. If you already have an advisor, you should send them this list of questions and ask for them to complete it **in writing**.

This list was created by Jason Zweig and published in the Wall Street Journal in 2018.

1. Are you always a fiduciary, and will you state that in writing?

> IMPORTANT: A fiduciary is someone that is legally obligated to put your interests above their own. For example, they shouldn't recommend Mutual Fund A that pays them a commission over Mutual Fund B if that is the better option. **You absolutely 100% should not hire an advisor that is not a fiduciary**. A non-fiduciary "advisor" is basically an insurance, annuity, or mutual fund salesperson. Avoid at all costs.

2. Does anybody else ever pay you to advise me and, if so, do you earn more to recommend certain products or services?

3. Do you participate in any sales contests or award programs creating incentives to favor particular vendors?

4. Will you itemize all your fees and expenses in writing?

5. Are your fees negotiable?

6. Will you consider charging by the hour or retainer instead of an annual fee based on my assets?

7. Can you tell me about your conflicts of interest, orally and in writing?

8. Do you earn fees as adviser to a private fund or other investments that you may recommend to clients?

9. Do you pay referral fees to generate new clients?

10. Do you focus solely on investment management, or do you also advise on taxes, estates and retirement, budgeting and debt management, and insurance?

11. Do you earn fees for referring clients to specialists like estate attorneys or insurance agents?

12. What is your investment philosophy?

13. Do you believe in technical analysis or market timing?

14. Do you believe you can beat the market?

15. How often do you trade?

16. How do you report investment performance?

17. Which professional credentials do you have, and what are their requirements?

SIDE NOTE: Professional credentials indicate the advisor has the education to back up their advice. You should prefer an advisor that has either the CPA®, CFA®, or CFP® designations. Others are good as well, but those are generally thought of as the "gold standards" for financial advice. Just because someone has one of these designations doesn't make them a good advisor, but it at least means they're good at taking financial tests. That can't be a bad thing.

18. After inflation, taxes and fees, what is a reasonable estimated return on my portfolio over the long term?

19. Who manages your money?

Once you get the list back, you should look for unsatisfactory answers.

If you find anything that makes you feel like the advisor doesn't really have your best interests at heart (question #1 being most important) – look elsewhere.

If you find that your current advisor doesn't fit the bill, look elsewhere. There are lots of competent, ethical, and highly qualified investment advisors out there.

Whether you end up hiring an advisor, buying some dividend funds, or managing it all yourself – you are in control of your financial destiny.

I sincerely hope that this book has given you some new ideas about investing and that it will benefit your investment results for many years to come!

ADDITIONAL RESOURCES

If you're still with me, thanks for joining. Really, thank you. There is a lot of information out there, so it means a lot that you read the entire book. I hope it was super helpful for you.

Here, I'd like to give you a few resources that will help you even more as you begin building your own Dividend Growth Machine.

The Dividend Growth Machine Newsletter (Free)

First off, you can sign up for the exclusive Dividend Growth Machine weekly newsletter. What is it? Well, each week I'll send you the most valuable content possible. You'll get one e-mail that has:

- Total read time under 60 seconds. You're busy. I get it. You don't have time to add 5,000 words to your already lengthy reading list. Don't worry, I want you to get the most value for the least amount of time invested.

- Links to one to five useful, practical, and/or interesting content from around the web. All content will be specifically relevant to you as a dividend investor. If you're here for recipes or cat videos, this isn't for you.

- A summary of each article. I'll summarize each article and pull out the main applicable points from each. Once again, you'll be able to read it all in a minute or less. I promise. Unless you're a slow reader, then -- well -- you should read faster.

It's free. And if at any time you decide you don't want to get the DGM newsletter, you can unsubscribe at any time at the bottom of each email.

Other Books ($3 to $20 Each)

If you want to read some more books, I would highly suggest the following:

- "The Essays of Warren Buffett" by Warren Buffett and Lawrence Cunningham. You'll get better advice here than just about anywhere else. An absolute **must read** by any investor or business person, for that matter. You can find all of these free in Warren's letters to shareholders for Berkshire Hathaway, but I find it helpful to have them summarized into topics.

- "The Snowball Effect" by Timothy J. McIntosh — a very interesting historical look at investing, markets, and dividend stocks.

- "The Single Best Investment" by Lowell Miller — a much better book than this one (honestly, it is) about dividend investing. He offers some useful tips on building your portfolio. It's a bit dated (2006) but is worth your time.

- "One Up on Wall Street" by Peter Lynch — not a dividend book, but a classic on investing.

- "The Intelligent Investor" by Benjamin Graham — the father of Value Investing (of which dividend investing is a close cousin). It's a bit technical, so I would recommend reading a few others before diving into this one, but it's a classic and another must-read for any serious investor.

I hope you enjoyed this book. Thanks again for reading and I hope to hear from you soon!

CONTACT ME

Thank you again for reading my book. Please send me an email at nathan@nathanwinklepleck.com. I would love to connect with you and hear what you think about the dividend strategy.

As a self-published author, I rely heavily on reviews to demonstrate quality to new readers. If you enjoyed this book, please take a few minutes leave your honest review on Amazon. It will only take a few seconds, but will help me out tremendously.

ABOUT THE AUTHOR

Nathan is a Portfolio Manager at Donaldson Capital Management, a fee-only registered investment advisor located in Evansville, IN.

Nathan earned his Bachelor of Science in Business Administration with concentrations in Finance and Economics from the University of Evansville. He is a Chartered Financial Analyst (CFA®).

When he's not helping people dominate their finances, he enjoys cheering for the Indianapolis Colts, avoiding spiders, and hanging out with his family.

DISCLAIMER

The information in this book is available as a service to its customers and other visitors, to be used for informational purposes only.

While we have tried to provide accurate and timely information, and have relied on sources we believe to be reliable, the book may include inadvertent technical or factual inaccuracies. The author does not warrant the accuracy or completeness of the materials provided, either expressly or impliedly, and expressly disclaims any warranties or merchantability or fitness for a particular purpose.

Neither the author nor any third party vendor, will be liable or have any responsibility for any loss or damage that you incur in the event of any failure or interruptions of this site, or resulting from the act or omission of any other party involved in making this site or the data contained in it available, or from any other cause relating to your access to, inability to access, or use of the site or these materials.

Decisions based on information contained on this site are the sole responsibility of the user, and in exchange for using this site, you agree to hold **the author** harmless against any claims for damages arising from any decision you make based on such information.

Nothing contained in this book should be used or construed as an offer to sell, a solicitation of an offer to buy, or a recommendation for any security. Nor is it intended as investment, tax, financial or legal advice. Investors should seek such professional advice for their particular situation.

This site is published in the United States for residents of the United States. Investors outside of the United States are subject to securities and tax regulations within their applicable jurisdictions that are not addressed on this site. Nothing on this site should be considered a solicitation to buy or an offer to sell shares of any investment in any jurisdiction where the offer or solicitation would be unlawful under the securities laws of such jurisdiction. U.S. investors are advised that not all investments described on this site are available for sale in all states.

Performance information presented on this web site is historical, and is not indicative of future results.

Investment returns and principal may vary, and at the time of sale, your investment may be worth more or less than its original cost. It is possible to lose money by investing in these funds. These investments are not deposits or obligations of or guaranteed or endorsed by, any bank, and are not federally insured or guaranteed by the U.S. government, the FDIC, the Federal Reserve Board or any other agency. Exchange-Traded funds frequently trade at a discount to their net asset value.

Municipal investments offer income free from federal income tax. Distributions may be subject to state and local taxes and to the alternative minimum tax. Capital gains will be subject to capital gains taxes.

Some featured products invest in international securities, which can involve different risks than U.S. investments. These risks include political or economic instability, difficulty in predicting international trade patterns, lack of publicly available information about foreign companies, changes in foreign currency exchange rates and the possibility of adverse changes in investment or exchange control regulations.

Some of the investments discussed in this book may not be available in or appropriate for a retirement savings plan.

Please contact your financial advisor about any investment restrictions associated with your particular plan.

You should contact a fund sponsor with specific questions about that sponsor's funds.

COPYRIGHT

Made in the USA
San Bernardino, CA
21 January 2020